Sister Mary Philip was born Mary Hardman in 1879, the youngest of five daughters born to John Hardman Jr. and his first wife, who died shortly after Mary was born. Her father was the owner of Hardman & Co., an ecclesiastical furnishings company in Birmingham, England. His company worked extensively with Augustus Welby Pugin in designing and producing stained glass windows, most notably those found in the Houses of Parliament. The Hardman family lived near Newman's Birmingham Oratory and eventually gave 6 nuns to the Church, all of different orders.

Mary Hardman entered the Bar Convent in 1905, taking the name Sister Mary Philip. Over the years, she developed a debilitating sensitivity to noise; nevertheless, she followed in the footsteps of many of her sisters in Religion at the Bar Convent—including Mother Mary Loyola—in writing extensively, including a monumental history of the Institute of the Blessed Virgin Mary, which sadly was never published.

She was trapped at the Institute's House in Rome when World War II began and was forced to stay until 1946, after the war ended. She died in 1963 at the age of 84, with over a dozen published works.

# THE SACRED HEART AND MINE IN HOLY COMMUNION

Thoughts drawn from the
Titles of the Sacred Heart
and the Writings of
St. Margaret Mary Alacoque

by

## SISTER MARY PHILIP

With a Preface by

## MOTHER MARY LOYOLA

2017

ST. AUGUSTINE ACADEMY PRESS
HOMER GLEN, ILLINOIS

This book is newly typeset based on the edition published
in 1920 by Burns, Oates & Washbourne. All editing strictly
limited to the correction of errors in the original text and minor
clarifications in punctuation or phrasing. Any remaining oddities
of spelling or phrasing are as found in the original.

*Nihil Obstat:*

C. Schut,

Censor Deputatus.

*Imprimatur:*

✠Edm. Can. Surmont,

Vic. Gen.

Westmonasterii,
Die 27 Maii 1920.

ISBN: 978-1-936639-82-3

# CONTENTS

# PREFACE

THE world rejoiced, as it might well rejoice, when the Treaty of June 28th, 1919, brought to a close the greatest conflict in its history. The victory on which its future so perilously hung was sudden and complete; the ideals of right and justice for which the Allies went to war were realized beyond all expectation.

Yet there was a note of profound sadness, almost of despondency, in the general exultation. It was not the huge task that remained to be done, the multitude of problems, political and social, still awaiting solution, which created depression; but the instinctive feeling that the very foundations of the structure to be laboriously raised were insecure. In a word, there was a deep-seated mistrust as to the lasting result of what had been bought at the cost of such heroic sacrifice.

The old order had changed, and men rejoiced, but they were distrustful of the new. "Unless the Lord build the city, they labour in vain that build it." And that the builders were labouring in vain, was said by many a warning voice. Not only was God left out of men's calculations, but His offers of guidance and help were rejected. Not only was His Name uninvoked, in official documents it was forbidden. And the result was the helplessness and discontent which found expression on all sides.

Father Faber described the sensation of dying as "all things sinking"—the dissolution of all the elements on which life depends. Something like this is the impression of many—and not pessimists, by any means—who reflect on the world of to-day. After rejecting Divine assistance and the principles which in earlier days were the acknowledged foundations of right and justice in the Christian commonwealth, men are left to grapple feebly with problems which elude them at every turn.

Not a few are seeking in union and organization the light and strength they need, whilst they turn a deaf ear to the reproach: "You will not come to Me that you may have life." There is a City set upon a hill as beacon to the nations. There is a Rock where men may find safety when all around is sinking. There is a

Voice which passes on from age to age with an infallible utterance the teaching of Christ, and alone proclaims the principles that must govern all legislation and reconstruction able to meet the needs and satisfy the legitimate aspirations of men.

This testimony of Christ to Himself and to His abiding presence in His Church, has never been more in evidence than in these days of ours. As the world grows older and the end draws nearer, it seems to His gracious purpose to disclose Himself ever more and more to all who have eyes to see. His revelations of Himself become more frequent, more intimate, more tender, as perils multiply and need grows more acute.

The revelation of His Heart is one which even Omnipotence cannot transcend. But it can be, and it has been, renewed and intensified, especially in times of stress and anguish such as the years of the Great War. How the widespread Arms and the pierced Heart have pleaded with God and man in the wayside crucifixes of ruined Belgium and northern France! How pressing was the invitation of the Sacred Heart to win its help by placing the arms of France under Its protection!

It has been said of God that He is patient because He is Eternal. The Church, the Bride of the Eternal, is patient, too. She can wait when her children are impetuous. She has postponed to our age, so sadly in need of fortitude and encouragement, the glorification of two heroines of France—the warrior Maid of Orleans, and the humble nun of Paray-le-Monial—unlike in every outward circumstance of their lives, yet with so much that is in common. Going back to the fifteenth century for one, and to the seventeenth for the other, the Church has brought them together to shine in the same radiance, and entrust them with the same message to the world: the message of trust in God and in the Name and the Heart of Christ.

It was with her victorious standard, inscribed with the Name *JHESUS*, that Joan led her troops to battle and saved her native land. It was the image of the Sacred Heart, of which Margaret Mary was the apostle, that—on the banner of France, and the uniform of many of her soldiers—checked the course of the invader and was the presage of Victory for the cause of the Allies in the Great War.

Fitly, then, has Sister Mary Philip given us once more the story of the Saint of Paray-le-Monial, supplemented now by a little book which sets before us in touching words the main claims of this Sacred Heart to our worship, our affection, and our trust.

The various invocations of the Litany, with the words of St. Margaret Mary skillfully interspersed, lend themselves admirably to Preparation for, or Thanksgiving after, Holy Communion. With this object in view, it may be confidently commended to those who welcome whatever may increase the glory, and further the interests of the Divine Heart, and who, sharing Its interests, may hope to feel the full effect of Its promises.

"And I, if I be lifted up," He said long ago, "will draw all things to Myself."

That first lifting up in torment and in ignominy is gratefully recalled in many a war-shrine throughout England; recalled, too, by that Enthronement of the Sacred Heart which our Holy Father earnestly desires to see taken up in families that it may be the salvation of the Home menaced by many dangers; recalled, also, by the solemn consecration of kingdoms to the Sacred Heart.

May that Divine Heart accept, in place of the official recognition refused elsewhere, the loving homage and reparation of Its servants! May It vouchsafe to bless and strengthen the League of Nations, and lead to the one divinely appointed centre of a united Christendom, the Apostolic See of Rome, the hearts of all who long for the security of supernatural authority and the strength of union with which to approach the questions of the day; that united once again in the Heart of God made Man, men may find that rest for their souls which they seek in vain elsewhere.

M. M. LOYOLA
St. Mary's Convent, York.
August 15th, 1919.

# I

## HEART OF JESUS,
## INFINITE IN MAJESTY
## AND MOST WORTHY OF ALL PRAISE

EACH time I receive Holy Communion, I hold within my heart the Infinite Majesty of God. It is true that Our Lord in His love for me, veils the splendour of His glory from me, for I could not look upon it and live. When He showed Himself in glory to His Apostles at the Transfiguration, they were so overcome that they "fell upon their face and were very much afraid" (Matt. 17:6). Therefore Christ comes to me under the white veil of the Sacramental species so that I may not fear to approach Him.

What a thought this is to fill me with humble astonishment and love!

He, the Infinite God, comes to me; He consents— He even delights—to dwell in my heart so full of faults and imperfections, so spoilt by past sins, so empty of all the adornments of virtue, so poor a place in which to entertain the Lord of Infinite Majesty. His love for me makes Him forget, and lay aside, the glory of His power and beauty, the might of His eternal splendour; but this should only be a most powerful incentive to me to greet the Lord of glory with all possible praise and reverence when He comes to dwell with me. No praise or homage that I can ever give Him will be adequate, yet will I do what I can, raising my heart in songs of love and praise, mingled with my awe and adoration.

Praise is the highest form of prayer. It is the prayer we shall use throughout eternity; it is the prayer which rises most surely from our hearts when we think of the Sacred Heart as *Infinite in Majesty and most worthy of all praise.*

Holy! Holy! Holy! Lord God of Hosts! Heaven and Earth are full of the majesty of Thy glory! I adore thee; I praise Thee; I bless Thee; I glorify Thee; I give Thee thanks for Thine own great glory! Heart of Jesus, Infinite in Majesty, I adore Thee, I thank Thee, I worship Thee. I bow myself down before Thee present in my heart in Holy Communion, and I humble myself to the utmost of my power before Thee. I acknowledge Thy Majesty, Thy power, Thy greatness. Lord, let me lose all thought of self, that I may be wholly taken up with the thought of Thee!

> O Sacred Heart! Thou Sunshine of our days,
> Be Thine the songs of everlasting praise,
> Whose strains shall break upon the eternal shore,
> Where we may love and praise Thee evermore!

## II

### Heart of Jesus, Glowing Furnace of Charity

OUR Lord often revealed Himself to Saint Margaret Mary, and showed her His Heart as a Furnace of love with flames issuing from It. Thus she writes:

"Jesus Christ my Divine Master appeared to me, resplendent with glory, His Five Wounds brilliant as live suns. Flames issued on all sides from His Sacred Humanity, but especially from His adorable Breast, which resembled a furnace. In this He showed me His most adorable Heart, the living Source of these flames. Then He disclosed to me the ineffable wonders of His love, and to what an excess He had carried it in His love for men, from whom He received only ingratitude. '*This,*' He said to me, '*I feel more deeply than all I suffered in My Passion. If they would return Me love for love, I should think but little of all that I have suffered for them, and should wish, if it were possible, to suffer still more. But, instead of love, I meet with coldness and repulse on every side, in return for all My eagerness to do them good.*'"

On another occasion the Divine Heart was represented to her as on a throne of fire and flames, shedding rays of light on every side, brighter than the sun, transparent as crystal. And again, as she approached Holy Communion, Our Lord showed her His Sacred Heart under the symbol of a burning furnace.

It is this same Divine Heart that I have in the Holy Eucharist, that Heart burning with love for me; and surely my heart, cold though it be, must be attracted and drawn to the Heart of Christ as by a strong magnet. When Our Lord comes to me in Holy Communion, His Heart actually beats in mine; my heart and His are united; I am surrounded, enveloped on all sides by His love—He in me, and I in Him, so that I can truly say: "I to my Beloved, and His turning is towards me." (Cant. 7:10) All my sins and imperfection can be burnt away, consumed utterly by the fire of His love if I but wish it.

Lord! I do wish it. Purify me completely! Let Thy love consume everything in my soul that is displeasing to Thee!

Then, when I am close to Him in Communion, the heat of His loving Heart will enkindle love in me. Frequent contact with His Heart, the Furnace of Love, should altogether change my heart. I, too should be filled gradually with the fire of love—love for the souls of others; love of all for His sake; love for sinners, for pagans, for infidels, for heretics, for all who do not know Him; love, especially, for those who know Him not and love Him not, that I may plead earnestly with the Heart of Christ for them; love for the sad, the poor, the depressed and downtrodden, the unsuccessful; love for the Church of Christ and our Holy Father, for Bishops and Priests, for Missioners and all religious. My love, my interests, my prayers should include all these; but I must not forget that I have nearer duties still, to my immediate neighbors, those with whom I live, all with whom I come in contact.

Yet even after my frequent communions how cold I am! how selfish! often how unkind, nearly always careless and unfeeling!

*O Heart of Jesus! Glowing Furnace of Charity!* Let the flames of Thy love change my heart and kindle within it the fire of Thy love. Warm my heart by contact with Thine own, so that I may love Thee, my Lord and my God, with my whole heart, and soul, and mind, and strength, and my neighbour as myself, for Thy sake. *Amen.*

# III

## HEART OF JESUS,
## CENTRE OF ALL HEARTS

IT IS easier to understand than to express all that is contained in the words: *Heart of Jesus, Centre of all Hearts*.

Apart from Christ, my heart can never be at rest. "Thou hast made me for Thyself, O Lord, and my heart can never be at rest until it rest in Thee," are the words of St. Augustine, and they find their fulfillment in the experience of everyone. The Sacred Heart of Jesus is the centre to which all hearts are attracted—there and there alone shall I find true rest. "Come to Me and you shall find rest for your souls." (Matt. 11:28) are Our Lord's own words. Woe, then, to me if I allow myself to be withdrawn from my true Centre by the false attractions of aught else.

Saint Margaret Mary, who felt an overwhelming attraction towards the Eucharistic Presence of her Lord, on one occasion tried—in compliance with what she thought was the wish of her Superior—to force herself to remain away from the Chapel during the time of Exposition. Our Lord reproved her severely:

"*Know that if thou withdrawest thyself from My Presence,*" He said, "*I will make thee feel it as well those who are the cause of it*"—and yet the Saint was doing violence to herself in resisting the attraction she longed to obey. What, then, can I expect if I willfully resist the sweet attraction of the Sacred Heart, and turn away to follow that of some paltry pleasure or gain? Surely, rather, will I give myself up wholly to the drawing of His love, and make Him in very truth the Centre of my heart, my life, my affections, my entire being.

If Christ be the Centre of my life, then will all my thoughts revolve round Him: I shall be anxious for His glory, zealous for His cause, keen to carry out His slightest wish. Then shall I delight in hearing of all that concerns Him, His triumph over the hearts of men, the spread of His Kingdom on earth. Then, too, will my words turn on Him, for "Out of the abundance of the heart the mouth speaketh." (Luke 6:45) And I shall put myself to all discomfort, and brave all human respect, if I may but help to gain one heart for Him.

If Christ be the Centre of my heart, I shall find all my joy, all my peace, all my delight, all my rest in Him. My life will move within the burning circle of His love, and by the Divine heat be purified and made beautiful.

O Heart of Jesus, Centre of all Hearts! Centre of my heart, grant that I may ever rest in Thee! Grant that all my thoughts, words, and actions may ever begin from Thee, and by Thee be happily ended. Let me never be led away from Thee by the false attractions of any creature; but do Thou draw me powerfully to Thee that I may be unable to resist Thy divine attraction, and yielding myself up to Thee, with all the affection of my heart, be forever united to Thee. *Amen.*

# IV

## HEART OF JESUS,
## FULL OF KINDNESS AND LOVE

WHEN I receive Holy Communion, I know that Our Lord comes to me with His Heart *full of kindness and love.* He does not come to overawe me with His majesty, His greatness, His power. He does not think of the infinite condescension that is His in coming to me. He does not consider His dignity or His rights. He comes simply *for me!* because He loves me, because He knows He can do me good, and because He longs to do it. All His thoughts about me are kind thoughts, appreciative thoughts, even—He always makes allowances, He understands always.

O kind loving Heart of my Lord! I adore Thee, I love Thee, I desire Thee! Would that I could make Thee some return for all Thy goodness to me! If I could realize more Our Lord's love of me, all my life would be strengthened and sweetened; I should be impelled by the very force of His love to love Him in return; I should glory in His love, and long to increase it, and desire it ardently. His love is, after

9

all, the one thing necessary. Having that I have all—and I have it!

Dear Lord, I believe; I thank Thee. Help me to Realize Thy love more and more! Let the thought of it transform my life; let it win me to whole-hearted service, to generosity, to fidelity in the smallest details. "Love is repaid by love alone." "Love is not loved!" My Lord! My King! Let this be so no more; let me love Thee in deed and in truth—love Thee always, and let everything else go.

Our Lord's Heart, *full of kindness and love*, must overflow into mine. How is it that after being so many times united to Our Lord, I am still so unkind to others? so hard in thought and judgment?

Lord! pardon me. Let the kindness of Thy Heart overflow into mine! Let me so empty my heart of self that Thou canst live in me! Think Thy kind thoughts in me! Speak Thy kind words through me! Let me allow Thee to act through me, for Thou art *full of kindness and love!*

## V

## HEART OF JESUS,
## ABYSS OF ALL VIRTUES

"DEVOTION to the Sacred Heart," wrote Saint Margaret Mary to one of her novices, "is a devotion which consists much more in the imitation of His virtues than in prayers and other pious practices." Our Lord Himself seems to inculcate this, for on the one occasion recorded in the Gospel on which He actually spoke of His Heart, the words He said were: "Learn of Me, because I am meek and humble of heart." (Matt. 11:29) But Christ does not leave us alone to learn of Him: "Come to Me," He says; "Come, unite thyself to Me in Holy Communion, and so learn of Me, for My Heart is the Abyss of all virtues." Yes, in Holy Communion I have Our Lord Who has all things, Who possesses all things. All virtues in their fullness come to me with Him, and He allows me to draw freely from His Heart.

Love of the Heart of Jesus, inflame my heart!
Charity of the Heart of Jesus, fill my heart!
Strength of the Heart of Jesus, sustain my heart!
Mercy of the Heart of Jesus, pardon my heart!
Generosity of the Heart of Jesus, change my heart!

Meekness of the Heart of Jesus, reign in my heart!
Patience of the Heart of Jesus, subdue my heart!
Peace of the Heart of Jesus, calm my heart!
Recollection of the Heart of Jesus, absorb my heart!
Silence of the Heart of Jesus, teach my heart!

When we are together—His Heart to mine—
His virtues flow into me; but for this I must empty
my heart of other things—of pride, of worldliness, of
dissipation, of resentment, of self-love, of unkindness,
of hard judgments, of all the countless faults that are a
barrier to the inflowing tide of His virtues. The more
empty He finds my heart of these things, the more
generously He will fill it with His own perfections.

Each Communion, therefore, should see me
advanced in the work of self-conquest. Each
Communion should leave me more humble, more
patient, more charitable, and less attached to the world
and my own self-will. This is the true way of profiting
by my Communions. The best proof of gratitude I
can give Our Lord for His visits of love is to *allow* His
virtues to grow and increase in my heart, and greatly to
*desire* that they should do so. Our Lord ever rewards
sincere desires: "He hath filled the hungry with good
things," are Our Lady's words.

Saint Margaret Mary, in a passage showing how
all our needs can be supplied by trust in the Heart of
Our Lord, says among other things:

"If you are filled with pride and vain self-esteem, bury yourself in the Humility of the Sacred Heart. If you find yourself in an abyss of infidelities and inconstancy, go and hide yourself in the Constancy and Stability of the Heart of Jesus. If you find yourself in an abyss of agitation, impatience or anger, go and bury yourself in the Sweetness of the loving Heart of Jesus, so that He may render you meek and humble of heart. If you find yourself so weak that you fall at every step, go and bury yourself in the Strength of His Sacred Heart, and He will deliver you."

# VI

## HEART OF JESUS, KING OF ALL HEARTS

BY every right and title Christ is King—King of kings and Lord of lords. We have His own word for it. "Pilate therefore said to Him; 'Art Thou a king, then?' Jesus answered: 'Thou sayest that I am a king. For this was I born, and for this came I into the world.'" (John 18:37) But, as He had said a moment before, His "kingdom is not of this world." No! He reigns first over the hearts of men— He is King of all hearts. Yet how far men are from universally recognizing the Kingship of Christ.

That He will triumph finally we all know, but in the present how little some of us recognize His royalty! How seldom do we pray earnestly for the extension of His kingdom; yet it is the petition He Himself commanded us to use: "Lord, teach us to pray," pleaded the Apostles, and He said to them: "When you pray, say: *Father, hallowed be Thy name. Thy Kingdom come.*" (Luke 11:2)

It is recorded that Our Lord often comforted His servant Saint Margaret Mary with the words: "I will

14

reign in spite of My enemies and in spite of all those who oppose Me." And she rejoined lovingly: "O my dearest Lord, when will that happy hour come? In the meantime I place in Thy hands the defense of Thy own cause, whilst I will suffer in silence." After the first recognition of the Feast of the Sacred Heart in the Convent at Paray-le-Monial, in 1686, Saint Margaret Mary said to her novices: "I have nothing more to desire, since the Sacred Heart is known, and begins to reign in the hearts of others. Do what you can, my dear Sisters, that It may reign in yours for ever as your Sovereign Lord and Spouse."

Four years later she wrote: "After all, the Divine Heart will reign in spite of all who oppose Him, and satan and his followers will remain confounded. How happy are those whom He uses to help Him to establish His reign! It seems to me that He is like a king who does not think of giving rewards whilst He is conquering and overthrowing his enemies, but who gives them largely when he reigns victoriously on his throne. The adorable Heart of Jesus desires to establish the reign of His love in all hearts by ruining and destroying the reign of satan. It seems to me that He desires this so much that He promises great rewards to those who take part in this work according to the lights and means He gives them."

If Christ is the King of all hearts, He is King of my heart. How do I treat my King? Do I allow Him full liberty in the kingdom of my heart? Do I in all things bow to His Sovereign Will? Do I, when He comes to me in Holy Communion, enthrone Him in my heart, and offer Him the homage of my love and praise? Do I lay all at His feet, and acknowledge Him as my King and Sovereign Lord? Do I, forgetting myself—or rather, leaving myself to His royal care—plead with my King for other souls? Do I long for His reign to be extended? Do I, in a word, treat with Him as King over my own heart, and over the hearts of all His creatures?

My King and my God, I beseech Thee to reign over me entirely. I subject my whole being to Thee—my soul with all its powers; my body, with all its senses, my heart, with all its affections. Reign over me completely dear Lord; and reign in the hearts of all men, that owning Thee as King and Lord, we may serve Thee here in all fidelity, and praise Thee for all eternity. *Amen.*

# VII

### HEART OF JESUS,
### IN WHICH ARE ALL THE
### TREASURES OF WISDOM AND KNOWLEDGE

IN Holy Communion I am intimately united to Christ. He comes to me, opening His Heart to me, and inviting me to take freely of the treasures enclosed therein. Our Lord made this very clear to Saint Margaret Mary, for she writes:

"His Sacred Heart is a secret treasure, and His one desire is to open It to us that He may enrich our poverty. Therefore He has resolved to manifest His Heart to men, and open out all Its riches to them, so that all those who do what they can to promote His love and honour may be filled with the divine riches of His Heart." "For my part," she adds, "this adorable Heart is all my treasure. I confess that I have nothing but the Heart of my Lord Jesus Christ, and He often says to me: 'What wouldst thou do without Me? Thou wouldst be poor indeed!' Let us then seek in this Divine Heart all we need. His treasures last for ever, they are of infinite worth, greater than it is possible for me to express."

In Holy Communion I possess this Treasure within me. From It I can draw that true wisdom which will lead me to seek first the kingdom of God—that true knowledge of which Our Lord said: "This is eternal life, to know Thee the One True God, and Jesus Christ Whom Thou hast sent."

In Christ are hid, as St. Paul says, "all treasures of wisdom and knowledge." Who, then, can teach me the wisdom and science of the Saints as He can?— and the wisdom of the Saints is what we all need—"to be wise, as it behoves us to be wise"—wise in valuing all things at their true worth, wise in acknowledging our own utter ignorance and weakness. Such wisdom I shall draw from the Heart of Christ. He will teach me to realize that He alone is good, He alone holy, He alone the Lord from Whom all my strength must come. Learning this wisdom, and growing in the knowledge of His love and thought for me, I shall cast myself and all my cares on Him, and say with real conviction: "I can do all things in Him Who strengtheneth me."

"If you are an abyss of ignorance," said Saint Margaret Mary, "go and hide yourself in the Heart of Jesus, where you will learn to love Him and to do what He desires of you."

I adore Thee, Heart of my Lord, Treasure of my soul, rich store-house of wisdom and knowledge—I adore Thee and unite my heart to Thine, so that Thy wisdom may fill it and that it may grow in the knowledge of Thee. O Christ my Lord, give me of Thy riches, for I am poor and needy! Well mayest Thou remind me of my poverty without Thee! Yet I would rather have my riches in Thee than in myself. Thy Heart can never fail me: its treasures are inexhaustible. Having Thee, I possess all things; all that I hope for, here or hereafter, I find in Thee. Let this Communion so bind my heart to Thine that I may never more forget Thee! Be Thou forever my Treasure, for then my heart will never be withdrawn from Thy love. Hast Thou not said Thyself: "Where thy treasure is, there is thy heart also"?

# VII

## HEART OF JESUS,
## PIERCED BY THE LANCE

Within the cleft I'll cower
Of Jesus' wounded Side;
In sunshine or in shower,
Securely there I'll hide.

IT is thus that St. Bernard writes of the Wounded Side of Christ: "The Lord Jesus permitted His breast to be opened by the lance in order that this exterior wound of His Body might serve to reveal the secret of His Heart." (*Sixth Sermon on the Canticles*) The secret of Christ's Heart is His love—that love of which St. Paul says that it "surpasseth all knowledge" (Eph. 3:19)

And St. Bonaventure: "The opening of the Heart of Jesus is a proof of His ineffable clemency. No creature is capable of understanding such excess of love; the Angels and Saints are ravished at the sight of such unbounded love . . ."

One Friday, towards the end of the year 1673, Saint Margaret Mary received special proof of Our Lord's love. "After I had received my Saviour, He placed my mouth to the Wound of His Sacred Side, and held me close to Him for the space of three or four hours with delights I can never express: I heard these words frequently repeated: "Thou seest now that nothing is lost in trusting in My power, and that all is to be found in the enjoyment of Myself?'"

Another time Our Lord presented Himself to her all covered with wounds, and told her to look upon the opening in His Sacred Side, which was an abyss opened by an arrow of immeasurable length—His love. This, He told her, was the dwelling-place of those who love Him. There, they find two lives: one for the soul, the other for the heart. The soul finds the source of living waters, to purify it, and to give it the life of grace of which it had been deprived by sin; the heart finds a furnace of love, in which all other love is consumed. But since the opening is narrow, it is necessary to be humble and detached in order to be able to enter therein.

Lord Jesus, grant that by Thy grace I may become humble and detached, so that I may enter into Thy Sacred Heart and never leave Thee. Grant me Thy love and Thy grace, of which Thy pierced Side is symbol—for Love pierced Thy Heart, and shed Thy Blood, and the Water of grace flowed from the Wound in a cleansing stream. Grant me then a safe hiding place in Thy Heart, for there I shall find not only the cleansing Water, but the Blood which inebriates and the Wine that bringeth forth Virgins.

> Soul of my Saviour, sanctify my breast!
> Body of Christ, be Thou my saving guest!
> Blood of my Saviour, bathe me in Thy tide!
> Wash me, ye waters, flowing from His Side!
> Strength and protection may His Passion be;
> O Blessed Jesus, hear and answer me!
> Deep in Thy Wounds, Lord, hide and shelter me;
> So shall I never, never part from Thee.
> Guard and defend me from the foe malign:
> In death's drear moments make me only Thine:
> Call me, and bid me come to Thee on high,
> When I may praise Thee with Thy Saints for aye.
> *Amen.*

# IX

## Heart of Jesus,
## Of Whose Fullness
### we have all Received

I N the first chapter of the Gospel of St. John, we read that the Word made flesh is "full of grace and truth;" and, two verses further on, that "of His fullness we have all received." (John 1:14-16) And St. Paul, in his Epistle to the Ephesians, bids us "know also the charity of Christ, which surpasseth all knowledge, that you may be filled unto all the fullness of God." (3:19)

What is this fullness of God? We cannot completely understand the words, but this we know: that God is Love, and that the Heart of God the Son is the very Centre and Fountain of that love; so that when we speak of the "fullness" of the Heart of Christ, we mean His love—that love of which we can measure neither the breadth, nor the length, nor the height, or the depth.

Our Lord spoke of this love of His more than once to His servant, Saint Margaret Mary. He appealed to her, and to the world, by His love: "Behold this heart which has loved men so much that It has spared nothing, even to exhausting and consuming itself to prove to them Its love." Here I have Our Lord's own word telling me of the fullness of love which He has shed abroad in the world, giving without stint nor measure, according to the capacity of each human heart to receive it. Redemption, which is the result of Christ's love, is a gift free to us all; each of us can say with truth: "He loved me and delivered Himself for me." (Gal. 2:20)

In the Holy Eucharist He comes to each of us, so that no one can feel himself excluded—no one can say that he is cut off from the fullness of the Heart of Christ.

When Our Lord comes to me in Holy Communion, He pours the fullness of His Sacred Heart into my heart—His wisdom, His knowledge, His love, His compassion for sinners, His endurance—all the mighty virtues of the Man-God are at my disposal, if only I will open my heart to receive them, and empty my heart of the obstacles which bar the full-flowing tide of His love. It is my own fault if I receive but little of His fullness, for He excludes not one from His generosity: "Come ye all to Me, that of My fullness you may all receive."

My Lord Jesus, I come to Thee in Holy Communion that I may receive the fullness of grace and virtue. Thou hast all things; I have nothing, and am nothing; give me of the fullness of Thy Heart, give me Thyself, that though so late, I may at last live only by Thee and for Thee!

My God, let the fullness of Thy Heart flow out to all the world: to all the poor; to all in need, or sorrow; it to all those who are weary with the burden and heat of the day; to all labourers in Thy Vineyard. Give of the fullness of Thy mercy and Thy pardon to all sinners: to all those who, knowing Thee, love Thee so little; to all who disappoint Thy Heart by their lack of generosity, and by their continual halting on their way towards Thee. For all these and for myself, the least generous of all, I pray: Give us, Lord, of Thy fullness, and change us into loyal servants and disciples of Thy Heart. *Amen.*

> O Thou, Thou wounded Heart of pity deep,
> Through which my way lies to the Father's throne
> Teach me the love which rent that crimson path,
> Gave us Thy life, but made our pains Thine own.
> *(Rev. G. Bampfield.)*

## X

## HEART OF JESUS,
## PATIENT AND ABOUNDING IN MERCY

OUR Lord once said to Saint Mechtilde: "I assure you that there is no sinner, however great his sins may be, whom I am not ready to forgive at once, if only he repent sincerely of his sins." With these words before me, I can picture my Saviour turning to question me—pleading, as it were, His own cause in the midst of my heart: "My child, how long? how long? When wilt thou give thyself wholly to Me? I am thy God: when wilt thou trust Me? I love thee intensely, I am thy Friend: when wilt thou love Me? When wilt thou give Me thy whole heart, and be completely generous? My child, I have waited so long and so patiently for thee; I have suffered for thee; I have forgiven thee all; I have given thee so much. What more can I do for thee? Let the patient kindness of My Heart touch thy heart, and win it to My love. My child, do not scorn the love of thy God, thy creator. Do not slight the love of My Heart."

My God, my patient Friend, *O Heart of Jesus abounding in mercy!* I kneel before Thee and adore

Thee. I thank Thee from the bottom of my heart for Thy loving patience with me. Christ, my Friend, forgive me! Forgive me for my delays, for my meannesses, for my want of generosity, for my coldness! Forgive the slights I have offered to Thy adorable Heart! My God, if Thou wert not *patient and abounding in mercy,* I should despair of Thee ever consenting to accept me for Thy friend; I should feel that though Thou mightest forgive, Thou couldst never give me a place in Thy Heart. But Lord, Thou art Thyself, infinite in patient, tender mercy, and so I trust in Thee, not only for forgiveness for the past, but for strength to give myself up wholly to Thy love.

"O Heart of love, I place all my trust in Thee, for though I fear all things from my weakness, I hope for all things from Thy love."

*(An indulgence of 300 days is attached to this, the favourite aspiration of Saint Margaret Mary.)*

# XI

## Heart of Jesus,
## Source of Life and Holiness

IN this title we invoke the Sacred Heart as the Source of the spiritual life of our souls—of that life, the perfection of which is holiness. "I am come," Our Lord says, "that they may have life, and may have it more abundantly." (John 10:10). And David exclaims: "With Thee is the Fountain of Life." (Psalm 35)

To Our Lord then, I must go, if I thirst for this life of holiness, and the Centre whence flows that Fountain of sanctity is His Most Sacred Heart. In Holy Communion Our Lord is especially the life of my soul. During the moments when He dwells within me, I am, if I put no obstacles, being filled with the overflowing holiness of His Heart. Without the Blessed Sacrament, the Food of my soul, my spiritual life would soon come to an end. I should lose all energy, all hunger for spiritual things; I should become weak, tepid and negligent, and fall at once into innumerable faults.

Truly, Lord, Thou art my Life. O, be so ever more and more! Let me have no life apart from Thee! Give me Thy own Divine Life to take the place of the life of mere nature into which I so easily drift. Come, Lord Jesus, come and live in me, that with Thy love my heart consumed may be. Come, and live in me Thy life of prayer, of charity, of humility, of detachment and recollection. Come, and so live Thy life in me that I may truly be able to say: "I live now, not I, but Christ liveth in me." (Gal. 2:20).

In each Communion Our Lord, Who is the Holy of Holies and Holiness itself, comes to sanctify me. Apart from Him there can be no sanctity, for "None is good but one, that is God." (Mark 9:18) To the Heart of God, the Fount of Holiness, I must go that I may be sanctified by Him, and that He may cleanse me from my sinfulness, heal the diseases of my soul, and strengthen my weakness.

My God, how much I need Thee! It requires omnipotent power to make me holy—to make a saint of me! Thou dost come with that power in Holy Communion. Thy desire is to use it over my soul. Only one thing can stop Thee from using it: *my will*... Lord! I yield my will to Thee; take possession of it completely, that Thou mayest have full power to make me holy, to sanctify my body with all its senses, my soul with all its powers, my heart with all its affections. I desire to place no obstacle in Thy way, but to give Thee all, to yield Thee this—and this—

O Passion of Christ, strengthen me!  Lord, set my sinful heart in Thy Most Holy Heart!  Wash me in Thy Precious Blood!  Purify me; sanctify me; unite me to Thyself!  Give me Thy love and Thy grace, and then do with me what Thou wilt!

# XII

## Heart of Jesus, Victim of Sin, Atonement for our Iniquities, Bruised for our sins

THESE three titles, taken separately or together, are sufficient, surely, to touch the hardest heart. And yet, am I touched by them? How often I have heard them, and passed on unheeding? Christ, my Lord, take away my heart of stone, and give me a heart of flesh, that I may truly grieve with Thee over my own sins and the sins of the world!

Our Lord one day appeared to Saint Margaret Mary as He was when Pilate presented Him to the people, saying, *Ecce Homo!* He was covered with wounds and bruises; His Blood flowed from every part; He bore upon His shoulders a heavy cross. And sadly He said: "Will no one take part in My sorrow in the pitiable state to which I am reduced by sinners?"

Another time He said to her: "Thou must raise thy heart and thy hands to Heaven by prayer and good works, presenting Me continually to My Father as a Victim of love, sacrificed and offered for the sins of the whole world, placing Me as a rampart and sure fortress between His justice and sinners."

A little while afterwards, Our Lord again disclosed to her His Heart, torn and pierced with wounds. "See the wounds," He said, "which I receive from My chosen people." And again: "I have not found anyone to give Me a place of repose in this My suffering and sorrowful condition."

It was thus that Our Divine Lord sought the sympathy of His loving servant, and she responded fully to His demand.

Have I no sympathy to offer to my King?—He suffered for me as much as for Margaret Mary. In the silence of my heart do I never hear His Voice pleading for love and reparation?—"My child, receive Me into thy heart; do not be afraid. Come to Me with full confidence. I have forgiven thy sins; I have suffered for them; My Body was bruised and torn to make reparation for them. My heart was bruised with anguish, so that thy heart might hate sin and cling to Me. I have offered Myself to Our Eternal Father as the Atonement for all thy iniquities, the Victim to pay all thy debt. I have suffered all, endured all, for thee. Wilt thou not believe in My love? Throw thyself completely on My love, and let not My labour for thee be in vain!"

My God and my Lord, I thank Thee again and again that Thou hast pardoned my sins, that Thou

hast atoned for them, that Thou hast offered Thyself
as a Victim in my place.   How can I thank Thee
enough?   How can I ever love Thee sufficiently?
Lord, I adore Thee, I love Thee, I thank Thee now, in
this Communion.   Heart of my God, bruised for my
sins, I offer Thee my heart; bruise it with sorrow and
with love—sorrow for my past sinfulness, love for all
Thy boundless love of me.

> Heart, Who all my sins hast borne,
> Bruised, humbled, crushed, forlorn;
> Heart, Whom I have pierced with pain,
> Be Thou never wronged again.

# XIII

## HEART OF JESUS,
## SOURCE OF ALL CONSOLATION

THE Sacred Heart which has loved us with an everlasting love is the true Source of all Consolation. His love, if I only rightly understood it, would so transform my life that I should indeed perpetually rejoice in consolation. It was this love which made St. Paul to cry out: "I am filled with comfort: I exceedingly abound with joy in all our tribulation," (2 Cor. 7:4); and St. Catherine of Siena to repeat continually: "O Sweetness! O Love!" It urged Saint Margaret Mary to say again and again: "O how beautiful is the Beloved of my Soul! Why cannot I love Him?" One drop of consolation given by Christ to His holy ones was worth more to them than all the joys that earth could offer. The comfort that came from Him sustained them in all their work and sufferings. "Yet more, O Lord, yet more," cried St. Francis Xavier. "To suffer or to die," prayed St. Teresa. And still more heroic was the cry of another chosen soul: "Not to die, but to suffer." And all this was the fruit of the consolation they found in the love of Christ's Heart.

But it is not to His Saints only that Our Lord gives His consolation: He has promised it to all who are devout to His Sacred Heart. "I will console them in all their afflictions" are the words handed down to us in the revelations of Saint Margaret Mary. Foolish, indeed, I shall prove myself if, in my troubles, I do not turn to the One Source whence help and comfort flow. There are many sorrows, but there is none that cannot be assuaged by the love of Christ. There is no heart so forlorn that it cannot find comfort in the Broken Heart of Christ.

> Heart so pitiful to heal!
> Tender Heart so quick to feel!
> Heart so ready to forgive!
> Heart so grateful to receive!
> Sea of love without a shore,
> Be Thou loved and trusted more!

The truth of this universal consolation rests on His own blessed words: "Come to Me all ye that labour and are heavily burdened, and I will refresh you." (Matt. 11:28)

Holy Communion, the union of Christ's Heart with mine, is the one sovereign remedy for all sorrow, all anxiety, all the countless troubles, great and small, which beset us in this valley of tears. Why, then, is it that I seek from a tiny stream of earthly comfort that consolation which I can draw indefinitely from its true Source, the Heart of Jesus?

My God, it shall be so no more. I acknowledge Thee as my only King, my only Comfort, my only Friend. To Thee will I turn in all my sorrows; to Thy Heart will I come; and, in humble confidence, I will drink at the Fountain of Thy love and sweetness, the *Source of all Consolation*.

# XIV

## Heart of Jesus,
## Our Life and Resurrection

THIS is one of Our Lord's self-bestowed titles: "I am the Resurrection and the Life." (John 11:25) Saint Paul in writing to the Colossians (3:4) uses these words: "When Christ shall appear, Who is your life; then you also shall appear with Him in glory." And again and again Our Lord tells us that He is in very truth our Life both here and hereafter: "He that eateth My Flesh and drinketh My Blood hath everlasting life; and I will raise him up in the last day." (John 6:55) "He that eateth this Bread shall live for ever." (*ibid.*, 59) And in another place: "I am come that they may have life, and may have it more abundantly."

When thinking of the Sacred Heart as the *Source of life and holiness*, our thoughts dwelt especially on that union of our hearts with His, which forms what we call our interior or spiritual life. In this title we honour Our Lord more as the origin and source of that eternal life of glory of which the Blessed Sacrament is the pledge.

*O Sacred Banquet in which Christ is received, the memory of His Passion is renewed, the mind is filled with grace, and a pledge of future glory is given to us!*

Saint Thomas Aquinas, writing of the Blessed Sacrament, tells us that It "leads us to our everlasting home, and reanimates the body to eternal life;" so that not only will my frequent communions build up the life of my soul, and lead me to an ever closer union with Our Lord, but also raise me up to that enjoyment of the Beatific Vision which is Heaven.

So prayed Saint Thomas in his wonderful hymn to the Blessed Sacrament:

> "Jesu! Whom for the present veil'd I see,
> What I so thirst for, oh! vouchsafe to me:
> That I may see Thy countenance unfolding,
> And may be blest Thy glory in beholding.
> *(Fr. Caswall's translation.)*

# XV

## HEART OF JESUS,
## OUR PEACE AND RECONCILIATION

OUR Lord, appearing one day to Saint Margaret Mary, said to her; "Sinners shall find in My Heart an infinite Ocean of mercy." In these words all can find consolation, for which of us would dare to think that the word "sinner" has no personal application? No, all are sinners, and so, one and all, we can stir up our hearts to gratitude towards the faithful Heart of Jesus, Who is *our Peace and Reconciliation*.

It is especially in the Sacrament of Penance, perhaps, that I can realize how far-reaching is that love of Christ which surpasses all understanding. How often have I knelt in the tribunal of penance, and heard the words of absolution, and known that with those words the Fountain of Christ's Blood was loosed, and the healing stream flowed over my sin-laden soul, restoring it once more to life and peace? Surely here, more than anywhere else, I can see clearly how truly the Sacred Heart is *our Peace and Reconciliation*. How great a work of love is this!—the love of the Good Shepherd for the lost sheep, the love of the Father for the son that had gone astray.

O Sacred Heart! my *Peace and Reconciliation* in the Sacrament of Penance, I adore Thee, I love Thee, I thank Thee. I thank Thee for all the absolutions of my life. And I pray Thee, by all the love of Thy Heart, that Thy labour for me may not be in vain.

> O Hope of every contrite heart!
> O Joy of all the meek!
> To those who fall how kind Thou art,
> How good to those who seek!

But Our Lord does more than reconcile me to Himself in the Sacrament of forgiveness. In Holy Communion He gives me His peace, the fruit of our reconciliation. "Let not your heart be troubled nor let it be afraid" (John 14:27) are His words to me as He crosses the threshold of my heart; and so often, if I will only listen, I can hear His words above the storm of trouble and temptation which are well-nigh overwhelming: "Peace, be still!" "It is I, fear not."

Surely I should learn this at least from the contact of His Heart with mine—that there is no lasting peace apart from Him, that He and He alone can give me that true peace which the world can neither give nor take away.

O Heart of Christ! teach me to seek all my peace and happiness in Thee. Come to me in Holy Communion, and give me Thy peace that I may never look for peace save from Thee and in Thee.

# XVI

## HEART OF JESUS,
## LOADED WITH INSULTS

THE Latin invocation *Cor Jesu, saturatum oppro-briis* is much stronger than its English transla-tion—literally, the words mean "saturated" or drenched with opprobrium, with humiliations, with reproaches. As a sponge is soaked through and through with water, so was Our Blessed Lord saturated, as it were, by a sea of outrages and insults.

In the year 1674, Our Lord appeared to Saint Margaret Mary and showed her His Heart as on a throne of fire, flames shedding rays of light on every side. The Wound which He had received on the Cross was clearly visible. A crown of thorns encircled His Divine Heart, and It was surmounted by a cross. Our Lord made the Saint understand that these instruments of His Passion were symbols, and that His immense love for men had been the source of all the sufferings and humiliations He had endured for us; that from the first moment of His Incarnation all these torments and this ignominy had been present to Him, and that the Cross had been even from the first moment planted, as it were, in His Heart; that He had then, at once, accepted, in order to prove His love for us, all the humiliation, poverty, and suffering that His Sacred Humanity was to endure throughout His mortal life, and also the outrages to which His love would expose Him to the end of time in the Blessed Sacrament of the Altar.

At another time Our Lord said to the same Saint: "If men would return Me love for love, I should think little of all that I had suffered for them, and should wish, were it possible, to suffer still more. But instead of love I meet with coldness and repulses on every side, in return for all My eagerness to do them good. Do thou, at least, console Me by supplying for their ingratitude as far as thou art able."

Surely these last words of Our Lord to His friend should find an echo in the hearts of us all, for are we not all His friends? "I will not now call you servants, but friends." (John 15:16)

And yet, how dare I take Our Lord's pleading for love as addressed to me personally? Have I not been among those who have insulted Him, wronged Him, outraged Him?

My loving Lord and Master, I cast myself at Thy Sacred Feet and confess my wretchedness. Yes, Lord! I have sinned—I have insulted Thee, I, to whom

Thou hast given so much, to whom Thou hast shown such tender love. Lord, with my whole heart I repent! O that I could serve Thee all the days of my life! O that I could blot out the past by my fidelity and love now! "My child," Thou sayest to me, "as far as the East is from the West so far have I cast thy iniquities from Me. I will remember thy sins no more. This is what thou canst do—only now be faithful to My love; be faithful to Me and I will count thee among My friends, and thy love for Me will be as balsam to My outraged Heart." Lord! I am Thine to do with as Thou wilt: only bind me close to Thee by the bonds of undying love!

> Heart so holy, Heart so pure,
> Heart so patient to endure;
> Heart which all our sins hast borne,
> Bruised, humbled, crushed, forlorn;
> Heart which we have wrung with pain,
> Be Thou never wronged again.
>
> *(S. M. X.)*

# XVII

## Heart of Jesus, Salvation of those who Trust in Thee

ONE of the promises Our Lord made to Saint Margaret Mary was that He would bestow on all those devoted to His Sacred Heart, "all the treasures of love, mercy, grace, sanctification and salvation that It contains." And in a letter which she wrote to Mother Saumaise, in August, 1685, she records that Our Lord had made known to her that those devoted to His Sacred Heart "should never perish."

Over and over again in her writings the Saint urges all to trust in the loving Heart of Jesus, for trust is the outcome and, indeed, the proof of love: "If we want to please the Divine Heart, we must honour It with a loving confidence. The Heart of Our Lord will never abandon us unless we abandon Him first. The Heart of Jesus loves us and will never allow us to perish as long as we confide in Him; when necessary, He will make us feel His power. What have you to fear? The Divine Heart is a throne of mercy, where the most miserable are the best received, provided they present themselves through love."

In one of the best known of her letters, Saint Margaret Mary wrote: "The Sacred Heart desires us to address ourselves to Him, in all our necessities, with a humble and respectful yet great and filial confidence, giving ourselves up completely to His loving care." "Give this loving Heart more love than fear. Confide in His goodness, and try to correspond with His designs." Thus does the Saint to whom Our Lord revealed His Heart transmit the message of her Divine Master. It seems as though the great yearning of His Sacred Heart is to secure that all should trust in His love. To this end He holds out a most powerful inducement: "I will be their Salvation." And to bring it home to each individual soul, He says, as He comes in Holy Communion: "This day is Salvation come to this house." (Luke 19:9) "Trust Me, and I will be thy Salvation"—as if He would say, "Only trust Me and no enemy can hurt thee; I will save thee from them all."

How can I express all this means to me? To be freed from my enemies—to be saved—to be sheltered in His Heart for ever!

O Lord my Christ, save me, be my Salvation, my Saviour, my Refuge!

Most especially must I trust Our Lord in time of desolation and temptation. When tempted, to trust myself not at all and Him utterly is the one sure way of being victorious. Here, more than at other times, the Sacred Heart of Jesus is the *Salvation of those who trust in Him.* It shows much more love to trust Our Lord in the darkness than in the light; when things go wrong than when they go right. Our Lord's ways are hidden ways, and I cannot expect always to understand them. "My ways are not your ways, nor are my thoughts your thoughts." Yet it is, perhaps, just in these times of trial that my hope and trust waver.

O Lord my God, open Thy Heart to me that I may find in It secure Refuge in all my trials! Give me the fullest and most complete trust in Thy Goodness, that I may place all my hope in Thee, and find how truly Thou art the *Salvation of those who trust in Thee.*

# XVIII

## HEART OF JESUS,
## HOPE OF THOSE WHO DIE IN THEE

"HOW sweet to be judged at death by Him Who has been our Friend through life," was one of Saint Margaret Mary's favourite sayings. Devotion to the Sacred Heart is the easiest, and certainly one of the surest ways of preparing ourselves for a holy and happy death. We have Our Lord's promise to His servant that those who are truly devoted to His Heart shall find in It their "secure refuge in life, and especially in death." If our hope is founded on the love of Christ's Heart for us, then it rests on a solid foundation; anchored deep down in that Heart of love, it can moved by no temptation. From death to life we shall pass securely, upheld by the love of Him Who is to be our Judge.

One of the greatest terrors of death is loneliness—and each of us must face it. I shall have to go forth alone—no earthly friend can help me or come with me. One only Friend will never forsake me—Jesus. "When I walk through the midst of the shadows of death I will fear no evil, for Thou art with me."

(Psalm 22:4)  Yes, He will stay with me to the end, my one hope of salvation His Sacred Heart, The Source of that love of His which I know will never fail me.

O Christ my Lord, be Thou my Friend through life, that in death I may not be separated from Thee! Let me so love and honour Thy Sacred Heart on earth that I may die in the hope that Thou wilt Thyself be my Refuge, my Hope, my Salvation. Let not the words of Thy servant, so often repeated by her, be left unheeded by my careless heart; but let me experience with her that "it is sweet to die after having had a constant devotion to the Heart of Him Who is to be my Judge!"

# XIX

## Heart of Jesus, Delight of all the Saints

O N earth and in heaven, the Sacred Heart of Jesus is the *Delight of all the Saints.* Our thoughts go back through the centuries to the countless holy men and women, Saints of God, who have found all their comfort, all their joy, all their *delight,* in the Heart of Christ. So is it still, in this twentieth century of ours—the Sacred Heart is still the *delight* of holy souls, of thousands who know and love Jesus Christ: nay, this same Divine Heart is the *delight* not of Saints and holy ones only, but of many and many a struggling soul, of many and many a poor sinner whose one hope is in Its mercy and love.

When we think of the Saints, memory recalls swiftly the names of some of those who were specially devoted to the Sacred Heart. First and foremost there is the Queen of Saints, the Holy Mother of God, she whose whole life and love and being were centred on her Son. If to the Saints the Sacred Heart is a *delight,* assuredly He must have been so to His Mother in a far higher degree—and eternally, she finds her delight in

Him in Heaven. St. John the Evangelist, St. Bernard, St. Gertrude, St. Mechtilde, the Carthusian monks headed by Dom Lanspergius, St. Francis of Sales, and many and many another have had special devotion to the Sacred Heart. As for Saint Margaret Mary, we know her cry: "O my only Love, my only Joy, what can I wish for outside Thee? Thou art my All!" "Find all your delight in this Divine Heart," she urged again and again, and she certainly practised what she taught. "Are you in an abyss of sadness? Go and lose yourself in the joy of the Sacred Heart; there you will find a treasure which will cause all your sadness to disappear."

From earth I raise my thoughts to Heaven and there I find the Sacred Heart to be the *delight of all the Saints.*

> O Sacred Heart! all blissful light of Heaven,
> Rapture of Angels, beaming ever bright,—
> Ravishing joys, in rich and radiant splendour,
> Flow from Thy glory in torrents of delight.
> (Father F. Stanfield.)

I can feast my heart on that glorious scene, picturing it to myself and knowing at the same time that "eye hath not seen nor ear heard, nor has it entered into the heart of man to conceive what things God hath prepared for those that love Him." (1 Cor. 2:9) As I gaze in spirit on the joys of Heaven, I imagine I hear

Our Lord's voice reminding me that if I desire to join that glorious company of Saints who find all their delight in Him, I must make Him my delight while I am on earth: "My child, open thy heart wide and let Me fill it with My joy, My peace, My love, Myself. Let My Heart be thy delight, as It is the Delight of all My Saints. I am their All. In Me they find all they can, or do, desire. In Me are all their longings satisfied. And as I am all in all to them, so do I desire to be all in all to thee. I, alone, can satisfy thy heart which I have made for Myself. Let Me, then, be thy Delight. Let Me be thy Joy, thy Gladness, thy Pleasure, thy All."

"Delight in the Lord and He will give thee the desires of thy heart." (Psalm 36:4)

O Heart of Jesus, really present within me in Holy Communion, I greet Thee, I welcome Thee, I adore Thee. Thou art the Delight of all the Saints, and Thou dost come to me. My Lord, I thank Thee, I love Thee, I delight in Thy Sacred Presence in my Heart. I will "joy in God, my Jesus." I will make Thee always my Delight, my Joy, my Pleasure.

Lord, let me be willing and anxious to forgo every other delight that I may have Thee and keep Thee. Take all, Lord. Let me be wholly sacrificed to Thee! But give me Thyself, and be Thou alone my Delight for evermore! *Amen.*

## XX

### HEART OF JESUS,
### HOUSE OF GOD AND GATE OF HEAVEN

HEART of Jesus, *House of God!* and the House of God is my Home. . . . Heart of Jesus, *my Home!*

The word "home" speaks to me of affection and love, of intimate intercourse, of sympathy extending not only to great griefs but to the least of sorrows. There are no secrets in the family circle, but all within it delight in being of one heart and one soul with each other. So is it in the *House of God*, that Sacred Home, which is the Heart of Christ. There, in that Home of Love, I rejoice in the love and tenderness of God my Father; within its circle I find abundant sympathy and comfort, in all my needs; there I may converse intimately with Him Whom I love—my God, my Father, and my Friend. If I but dwell in His Heart, Our Lord will share in all my joys and sorrows, sweetening the one and lightening the other; yes, and if He find me faithful, He will let me have a part in His joys—and His sorrows, a far higher grace.

This is the Home Our Lord offers me each time He comes to me in Holy Communion—"My child," He said to Saint Margaret Mary, "My Heart will be to thee a sure place of refuge. Take care never to depart from It." To urge us to correspond with Our Lord's desire, we may listen to the burning words of His servant: "What happiness to belong entirely to the Heart of Jesus—to dwell there, and to draw therefrom the foundations of all perfection! There the soul tastes the sweet reign of unalterable peace, and looks upon all the vicissitudes and troubles of life without being upset by them and without being troubled by those things which pass like a dream. Let us then establish our actual and perpetual dwelling in the loving Heart of Jesus. There, together with this steadfast peace, we shall find strength to make our good desires effectual, and grace never to offend Him by any willful fault. Let us take to the Sacred Heart all our troubles, our bitterness, even our annoyances: He will shed His peace over all. There we shall find the remedy for all our evils, strength in weakness, and a place of refuge in all our necessities, for all that comes from that Divine Heart is sweet; He changes all into love."

Oh! God of Love, open Thy Heart to me in this Communion. Open to me this Home of love, from which, once having entered, I may never withdraw myself!

> O! Mary, by the priceless love
> Which Jesus' Heart bore Thee,
> Pray that my home in life and death
> That loving Heart may be.

Shelter me in life, my Lord, and let death find me still enclosed in Thy Heart, *the House of God;* then, indeed, Thy Heart will be to me the *Gate of Heaven* and I shall rest in Thee for ever.

> Heart of Jesus! broken Heart!
> Praise and thanks for all Thou art!
> Shelter in the noonday heat,
> Covert when the rain doth beat,
> Home where all find peace and rest,
> Be Thou known, and loved, and blest!
>                                    *(S. M. X.)*

# XXI

### Heart of Jesus,
### Fountain of Sweetness

OUR Lord once said to St. Catherine of Siena: "Daughter, the place of refuge where you must abide is the cavern of My wounded Side. Enter there, and you will taste the sweetness of love, for in My open Heart you will find Charity."

Then the Saint communicated and experienced a sensible sweetness, which remained in her mouth for many days.

The Eucharistic Heart of Jesus is indeed a Fountain of Sweetness. "O taste and see that the Lord is sweet," sang Holy David (Ps. 33:9); and every time I assist at Benediction I am reminded that "He has given us Bread from Heaven, containing in Itself all sweetness." Each time I receive Holy Communion I am able to say: "How great is the multitude of Thy sweetness, O Lord, which Thou hast hidden for those who fear Thee!" (*Imit., Bk. IV, ch. xiv.*)

> We thank Thee—Oh! how can we thank Thee, Jesus!
> That in this Sacrament Thou art our food;
> That we can find all sweetness that may please us
> In this dear Banquet of Thy Flesh and Blood!
>
> *(S. M. X.)*

When the Sacred Heart, the *Fountain of Sweetness,*
rests within my own heart, I can beg of Him to let
the sweetness of His love overflow into mine. From a
Fountain I can draw perpetually without any fear of its
running short: so, to the Heart of Christ I can come
again, and again, and draw Its sweetness into my own
bitter heart, that at last my King may be attracted by
His own sweetness to rest more and more intimately
with me—sweetening all my life, and turning its
sorrows into joys, its pain into pleasure, its loneliness
into perfect friendship.

To the *Fountain of Sweetness,* too, I can have recourse
for others. I can ask Our Lord to sweeten the burden
of the Holy Father, of Bishops and Priests, of all
who toil in His Vineyard. To Him I can commend
Missioners, that their hard and lonely life may be
lightened and sweetened by the Sacramental Presence
of their Lord. To His Sacred Heart I can bring all
religious, that their lives of prayer and penance and
toil may be rendered sweet by the thought of the Lord
whose spouses they are. Then there are the poor, the
unsuccessful, the heavy laden—they, too, must be
brought to the *Fountain*, that they, too, may taste and
see how sweet is the Lord. Lastly, there are sinners
without number, all dear to the Heart of Christ: for
these, too, I must plead that, before it be too late, they

may repent and find for themselves how truly He spoke when He told them that His "Yoke is sweet."

Lord Jesus, Thy desire is to sweeten the lives of all. Listen, then, to my prayer for these intentions of Thy Heart. Let Thy sweetness, of which that Heart is the *Fountain and Source,* flow over all the world. And for myself, let me ever remember that all sweetness for my body and soul is contained in that delicious Bread, which is Thy Body and Blood.

> Sweet Sacrament, I Thee adore!
> Oh! make me love Thee more and more!

# XXII

## Heart of Jesus,
## Strong Fortress from our Enemies

"THE life of man is a warfare," wrote Holy Job. No one can pass through life without combat. I must not expect to be without attack from enemies, especially if I have resolved to serve God generously. "My son," says the Wise Man, "when thou comest to the service of God, prepare thy soul for temptation." This is a dreary outlook. But in Holy Communion, Our Lord gives me a sure place of refuge, even the *Strong Fortress* of His Heart.

There I can hide myself, there I shall be safe—safe, in the first place, from the anger of the Eternal Father, which I have so justly merited by my sins. From the Citadel of the Heart of Jesus I can say: "Father, look not upon me, but upon the Heart of Thy Christ, and for His sake pardon my iniquities."

In the Sacred Heart I shall be safe from my enemies, also.

> O good Jesus, hear me!
> Within Thy Heart hide me!
> From the malignant enemy defend me!
> Never permit me to be separated from Thee!

"Keep yourselves hidden in the Sacred Heart of Our Lord," said Saint Margaret Mary; "hide your weakness therein as in a *strong Fortress*. Above all, take refuge therein when you feel yourselves attacked by the enemies who reside within you; they desire to discourage and trouble you at the least difficulty; but in the Sacred Heart you will find strength sufficient to keep you from all trouble and discouragement. Fidelity to this practice will keep your souls in peace."

Dear Christ, my Lord, open to me Thy Sacred Heart, that *Strong Fortress* wherein I shall be secure from every danger, and protected from all my enemies. Open Thy Heart to me, and when once I have entered in, close the Citadel and imprison me within it! Bind me there by the bonds of love—for there only can I find peace, there only can I know true security.

> Oh! Take me to Thy Sacred Heart
> And seal the entrance o'er,
> That from that home my wayward soul
> May never wander more.

# XXIII

## HEART OF JESUS,
## SCHOOL OF DIVINE LOVE

WHEN in Holy Communion Our Lord visits me, He invites me to enter the School of His Heart, there to learn the true science of His love. "Enter the Sacred Heart of Jesus," says Saint Margaret Mary, "as a disciple of the *School of Divine Love*. Leave and forget all worldly folly, self-love and vanity, so that you may be wise only in the science of pure love."

Follow eagerly and generously the Voice of Christ which says: "Come to Me you who desire to love Me, and I will lodge you in the School of My love, where you will become meek and humble of heart. Thus will you find the peace and rest of this same love."

In Holy Communion Christ is especially our Master. "You call Me Master and Lord, and you say well, for so I am," (John 13:13) He says to us—and the lessons of His Heart, the *School of Divine Love,* are all taught by Himself. What folly is mine if I do not try to learn the lessons He would teach me in my frequent Communions! What folly to refuse to enter myself among His faithful disciples! And yet how little have I learnt of His ways!

Each time I receive Christ into my heart, He repeats His loving invitation: "Come to Me all you that labour and are heavy laden, and I will refresh you. Learn of Me for I am meek and humble of Heart." If I love Him truly I shall desire to imitate Him, to be like Him—for devotion to His Sacred Heart consists, according to Saint Margaret Mary, "far more in trying to imitate His virtues than in prayers and exterior practices." And in this Science of the Saints, this Science of loving imitation, Our Lord Himself deigns to be my Master. I am too dear to Him for Him to entrust the work of teaching me to another; Himself, He comes, and opening His Sacred Heart to me, bids me enter and learn there the lessons I can learn nowhere else.

My Lord and Master, open Thy Heart to me that I may enter into the *School of Divine Love,* and learn that Science which alone is necessary. Teach me Thy lessons, dear Lord; enlighten me to understand them; and give me strength and grace to put them into practice. Oh! patient Heart of Jesus, weary not of Thy task of teaching me. Let each Communion make me more and more docile, and more and more in earnest in my endeavour *to live* the lessons Thou deignest to give me in the School of Thy Heart!

# XXIV

## HEART OF JESUS,
## SUN OF OUR SOULS

IN Holy Communion I have Jesus Christ actually present within me. I can think of Him, the Light of Light, seated on the throne of my heart, showing His own Most Sacred Heart to me as a brilliant sun, shedding its rays on all around, and lighting up the darkness of my soul.

On more than one occasion Our Lord showed His Heart to Saint Margaret Mary under this appearance of a sun. "Once," she says, "during Exposition of the Blessed Sacrament, Our Lord showed Himself to me resplendent with glory, and with His Five Wounds brilliant as five suns." At another time, the Feast of the Visitation, 1688, "Jesus allowed me to taste joys which I cannot express. I saw a throne of fire, upon which was His adorable Heart, sending out rays on all sides, and more brilliant than the sun."

"On the First Fridays," she writes, "the Sacred Heart is shown to me as a sun, brilliant with dazzling light, whose rays fall straight on to my heart. These rays fall also on the hearts of others, but with different results. Those whose hearts were unrepentant became still more hardened—as mud under the action of the sun; but on the hearts of the just, the rays fell with a softening influence which made them as wax."

In Holy Communion Our Lord sheds His light upon my heart, and according to my love in receiving Him, His work is more or less active in me. Surely the heat of His love should melt even my coldness, and soften even my hardness. But is my heart really as wax in hands? Can He mould me as He wishes? Am I ready to bend to His Will in all things, in the small as in the great?

The Blessed Sacrament is the sun of my life. "As beauty of form and colour is derived from the ray of light, so all varieties of sanctity (the effects of grace) stream out from Jesus Christ as from the sun of the spiritual world. Grace is the ray; but the Sun whence that ray pours is Himself."

Dear Christ, my Lord, *Sun of Justice,* shed Thy divine rays upon my selfish heart, and with Thy love melt its hardness. Let me be no longer barren and unfruitful, but under Thy Divine influence let virtue grow and flourish in my heart. "Too late have I known Thee, too late have I loved Thee, Oh! Truth and Beauty ever ancient, ever new"—yet now at least I yield myself to Thee. Be Thou in very truth the light

and sunshine of my life! Be Thou my Pleasure, my
Contentment, my Joy for evermore!

> Oh! Sacred Heart, thou Sunshine of our days,
> Be Thine the songs of everlasting praise,
> Whose strains shall break upon the eternal shore,
> Where we shall love and praise Thee evermore!

# XXV

## HEART OF JESUS,
## FOUNTAIN OF LIVING WATER

OUR Lord said to the Samaritan woman: "If thou didst know the gift of God, and who is he that saith to thee, Give me to drink; thou perhaps wouldst have asked of him, and he would have given thee living water" . . . "the water that I will give him, shall become in him a fountain of water springing up into life ever lasting." (John 4:10 and 14) This water of life is divine grace, and the Fountain from which it springs is the Sacred Heart of Our Lord.

In one of the decrees which preceded the beatification of Saint Margaret Mary, we read: "The Redeemer of the world, who, lifted up on the Cross, will draw all to Him, marvellously attracted and drew to Himself His Servant Margaret Mary. He made her approach to His uplifted Heart, so that she could taste at its very source the sweetness of His infinite love, and so make it known among men."

Thus, the waters of sweetness which Margaret drew from the open Side of Christ were spread by her as by a river all over the world. Her great and only desire was to purify the hearts of men in this Ocean of living water, and to cause to spring up in them the Fountain of the Water of Everlasting Life.

Saint Margaret Mary herself writes: "Consider the Sacred Heart in the midst of your heart as a *Fountain of living water,* and ask Our Lord to water the garden of your soul, where the flowers of virtue are all faded. He will restore their beauty to them, so that your heart may once more become the garden of His delights." To Father Claude de la Colombière she said: "The Sacred Heart of our good Master is an abundant Fountain of Mercy, Grace, Love, and every sort of delight. It is a Fountain which flows with abundance for His friends, and He desires only to reach all souls, and especially the souls of those who are faithful to Him."

On one occasion Our Lady appeared to Saint Margaret Mary, and said: "Come and draw the waters of grace and salvation from the Divine Heart of my Son, for it is a source of inexhaustible blessings and grace."

And again the Saint writes: "Love will allow us to find all that we want in His Heart, for It is a Fountain from which the more one draws, the more abundant are the waters of grace that flow from it. This Divine Heart is inexhaustible. From It flow three streams: one, of mercy for sinners; the second, of charity for all in any distress, or necessity, and particularly for those who tend towards perfection, who will find in it grace sufficient to vanquish all obstacles; the third, of love and light for those more perfect souls who desire to be united to Him. The grace from this stream will teach souls the science of the Sacred Heart, so that they may consecrate themselves to Him and so glorify Him, each in its measure."

Heart of Jesus, *Fountain of Living Water,* I adore Thee, I love Thee, I give myself up to the influence of Thy grace. Cleanse my heart, I beseech Thee, that I may be less unworthy of Thee. Purify my actions, my words, my thoughts, my motives of action, all the inmost workings of my soul. Wash me yet more from my iniquity, and cleanse me from my sin. And then refresh me, dear Lord, with the pure waters of Thy love, that my soul may never thirst again for aught that is less than Thee.

> O Fount of endless life!
> O Spring of water clear!
> O Flame celestial, cleansing all
> Who unto Thee draw near!

# XXVI

## Heart of Jesus,
## Altar of Sacrifice

O Heart of Jesus, purest Heart,
Altar of Holiness Thou art;
Cleanse Thou my heart, so sordid, cold,
And stained by sins so manifold.

ACCORDING to Our Lord's own words we are all called upon to sacrifice self in His service. "If any man will come after me, let him deny himself." (Matt. 16:24) Each time Our Lord draws near to me in Holy Communion, He asks me *to give myself up to Him,* that is to sacrifice myself: "My child, give Me thy Heart." Now, if I am to be a victim offered to Christ, I must have an altar upon which my holocaust may be consumed, and Our Lord points to His Heart, and invites me to offer myself there in union with His own sacrifice of love.

"Place yourself in the Sacred Heart," wrote Saint Margaret Mary, "as a victim to be immolated. The flames of love from this Divine Heart will consume your heart as a holocaust, so that nothing of self remaining, you may be able to say with St. Paul, 'I live, now not I but Christ in me.' I act only for Him, and His Sacred Heart lives and acts in me. He loves for me, and supplies for all my defects."

When, in Holy Communion, I place myself upon the Altar of His Heart, I am not alone in my sacrifice, for on this selfsame altar Jesus offers Himself—the priceless Victim, the Holocaust of infinite value. "His thoughts, His words, His actions, His sufferings, His Body and Soul—all are offered up on the golden altar of His Heart for the Glory of God and the salvation of mankind." (*Rev. J. McDonnell, S.J.*)

In the Jewish Temple, there stood beside the Altar of Sacrifice the Altar of Incense, where the Sacred fire burned perpetually. This Altar, too, prefigured the Heart of Jesus; for from His Heart issue flames of burning love for mankind, and from It, too, rises the sweet incense of prayer, ever pleading in atonement for the sins of the world.

Upon the Altar of Thy Heart, my Lord, I place my soul with all its powers; my body with all its senses; my heart with all its affections—my whole being—to be given up and sacrificed to Thee. I offer Thee also my temptations, my doubts, my perplexities, my anxieties. To Thy service I consecrate all my thoughts, words, and actions—my time, my talents, my health, my whole life.

Deign, O Jesus, to accept my oblation in the odour of sweetness, and as Thou hast given me the desire and the will to make it, so also I trust in Thee for grace and strength to complete it. *Amen.*

# XXVII

## Heart of Jesus,
## Our Father

OUR Lord comes to me in Holy Communion as a most kind indulgent Father. In these visits of love, well may He remind me of all His claims to this title. He is my Creator, and He brought me forth on Calvary to a new life in the midst of suffering and sorrow. To me, as to His servant at Paray-le-Monial, Our Lord might say: "What dost thou fear? Can a child perish in the arms of her Almighty Father?" And the Saint, passing this lesson on to others, wrote: "Enter as a loving child into the Sacred Heart, there to be healed of the wounds made in your soul by your disobedience, vanity, and ingratitude to this good Father, who brought you forth on Calvary with pain so great that He is covered with wounds and blood. His only desire is to put you in possession of His Kingdom, to let you rest upon His breast as a child of love who gives himself up entirely to the care of His adorable Providence, and you will want for nothing, for He is all powerful. So abandon yourself without reserve to His love and give Him your heart. This is what He asks of you in order to make your life conformable to His. . . . Draw from His Heart the love of a child towards Him, the love of a father towards your neighbour, and the love of a judge towards yourself."

Each visit of Our Lord to my heart should increase my confidence in Him, for He is truly my Father, and has more than a Father's love and care for me. He will treat me as a loving father treats his child. Possibly, He may rebuke me—but rebuke, and even chastisement, will always be tempered by His love, for "Whom the Lord loveth He chastiseth: and He scourgeth every son whom He receiveth." (Hebrews 12:6)

O Heart of God, Heart of my Father, present within me in Holy Communion, I adore Thee, I love Thee, I worship Thee!

> No earthly father loves like Thee;
> No mother half so mild
> Bears and forbears, as Thou hast done
> With me Thy sinful child!

And so, my Father, I come to Thee with filial trust, with ardent love. I come to Thee and place my whole hope in Thy Divine Heart. To Thee I commit my past, my present, my future—my life, my death. To Thee I give myself with utmost love.

For the love of God is broader
Than the measure of man's mind,
And the Heart of the Eternal
Is most wonderfully kind.

# XXVIII

## HEART OF JESUS, OUR SHEPHERD

OUR Lord seems to have loved this title: "I am the Good Shepherd Who giveth His life for His sheep." And truly He has not only given His life for me upon the Cross—but He gives me Himself daily in His Sacramental life. When I have strayed from Him, He has never wearied in His search for me, nor has He left me in my misery, but He has lifted me up, and embraced me, and carried me back to the fold upon His shoulders.

"How frequently we should meditate," writes Saint Margaret Mary, "upon the steps our Sovereign Shepherd has made when seeking us! We should thank Him for all these steps of His, and beg Him to give us the grace to walk ever in the paths of His love, uniting all our steps to His. We may often say to Him: "My loving Shepherd, detach me from all earthly things and from myself, so that I may be united to Thee. Let me hear Thy voice, and do Thou draw my heart so powerfully to love Thee that I may be unable to resist Thee!""

How intimate is the love shown by the Sacred Heart of *Our Shepherd*. "I know mine, and mine know Me," He says—as though to reassure me, and bring home to me, that all my needs are known to Him; and that all my aspirations after better things, all my failures, all my longings are quite clear to Him—and as though to promise me that He will manifest Himself to me, if I am faithful in keeping near Him, in following Him, as my Shepherd. Surely, when, in Holy Communion, His Heart beats in mine and mine in His, I can safely rest in Him, abandoning myself entirely to His loving care. He knows my every want, He will never let me be in need, but He will be pleased if I cast all my care Him when He visits me, and forgetting myself, plead with Him for those other sheep of His that are gone astray, and for those, too, that are not of His fold—for His Heart yearns to gather them all into Its safe shelter. "And other sheep I have, that are not of this fold; them also must I bring, and they shall hear my voice, and there shall be one fold and one shepherd " (John 10:16).

Lord Jesus, my Shepherd, I adore Thee, I love Thee, I thank Thee for all Thy tender care of me. I trust myself, and all that concerns me, to Thy loving Heart; I abandon myself entirely to Thy Providence. Listen now, my Lord, while I plead with Thee for those countless sheep of Thine that stray far from Thee! Bring them back, O kind Shepherd, from the dark paths of sin, which lead to ruin. Gather them into Thy fold before the darkness closes around them. Remember that Thou hast shed Thy Precious Blood to save them from destruction. Have pity, Lord, have pity on all sinners! Forgive them, for in very truth they know not what they do!

> Jesu! Shepherd of the sheep,
> Thou, Thy flock in safety keep!
> Living Bread! Thy life supply;
> Strengthen us or else we die;
> Fill us with celestial grace,
> Thou Who feedest us below!
> Source of all we have or know,
> Grant that with Thy Saints above,
> Sitting at the feast of love,
> We may see Thee face to face!

# XXIX

## Heart of Jesus, Our Pilot

THE journey from earth to heaven is often likened to a voyage across the ocean—the Ocean of Life. As safety in the midst of the perils of the sea depends very much on the ship upon which I embark, Our Lord seems to invite me, in my spiritual voyage, to enter His Sacred Heart, and give myself up to His guidance, so that I may securely reach the Eternal Shore to which I am journeying.

"Enter this loving Heart," writes Saint Margaret Mary, "as a traveller into a sure ship, for Christ Himself is the Pilot who will conduct you safely over the rough sea of this world. He will preserve you from danger and from storm, that is, from all the suggestions of your enemies, your passions, your self-love, your vanity and attachment to your own will and judgment. This Divine Pilot will guarantee you against all these perils, so that you may make your way across a calm sea, and so arrive at the port of Salvation."

Again, in another place, the Saint exclaims: "Ah! if we could only understand how much souls advance when they are faithful in letting themselves be guided by the Divine Pilot in the vessel of His loving Heart. Let us give ourselves up absolutely to the care of this Wise Pilot, and do all our actions in the spirit of abandonment to His Providence. Often we may say to Him: 'My God, Thou art my All, my Life, my Love! Save me, and suffer me not to perish in the flood of my iniquities.'"

When Our Lord comes to me in Holy Communion I can hide myself in His Heart, and rest there securely, however much the waves of temptation and trouble beat upon my soul. If I cast my care upon Him, He will say to me as once to the affrighted Apostles, "It is I, be not afraid"—and quelling the storm with His gentle command, "Peace, be still!" He will say to me: "Why are ye fearful, O ye of little faith?"

My Lord, I desire nothing more than to give myself up completely to Thy loving guidance. Be Thou for ever the Divine Pilot of my soul! Jesu, Deliverer! Come Thou to me, and smoothe my voyaging over Life's sea! Be Thou, O Sacred Heart, the Ark in which I shall be saved from the waters, which at times come in even to my soul! Enclosed in Thy Heart, and with Thee for my Pilot, I can brave all dangers and weather all storms. "I will fear no evils for Thou art with me," and I know that Thou wilt guide me to the Port of eternal salvation.

Sweet Sacrament of Rest!
Ark from the Ocean's roar,
Within Thy shelter blest
Soon may we reach the shore.
Save us, for still the tempest raves;
Save, lest we sink beneath the waves;
Sweet Sacrament of Rest.

*(Father F. Stanfield.)*

# XXX

## Heart of Jesus,
## Our Friend

THE friendship of David and Jonathan is given to us by Holy Scripture as a type of perfect friendship. "The soul of Jonathan was knit with the soul of David, and Jonathan loved him as his own soul." (1 Kings 18:1) But what was the bond of their love for each other compared with the bonds of love which knit me to Christ our Lord? What friendship can compare with the intimate friendship He contracts with those who love Him? Our Lord is the *Friend* of all. No one need be excluded from the privilege of calling Him by that title—for the condition He exacts is not hard. "You are My friends," He says, "if you do the things that I command you"—"If you love Me, keep My Commandments." (John 14:15) But for those who desire it He holds out the promise of a much more intimate friendship than this. "Abide in Me. As the Father hath loved Me, I also love you. Abide in My love." (John 15:9) And for this intimate companionship the condition is fidelity, not only to His external commands but to that interior voice of love, which is ever calling for the minute observance of His Will and the generous sacrifice of self in His service. If I am ready to give Him this further proof of affection, then will He admit me to the intimacy of His love.

In every Communion I make, Our Lord offers me this friendship of His Heart—offers it to me no less than to His Saints, and on the same conditions: the Saints are the intimate friends of Christ just because they accept His conditions utterly and fulfill them faithfully. If I can only be as generous as they, I shall receive love for love no less than they. Then will all the aspect of my life be changed, for I shall truly love and know myself to be loved in return. The joy of my friendship with Christ will lighten every burden, soothe every pain, make beautiful all that is hard and dull and dreary. Saint Margaret Mary used to say that, having Christ for our Friend, we could tell Him all the secrets of our heart and speak to Him of all our miseries and needs. "O Friend of my heart," she prayed, "she whom Thou lovest is ill. Visit me and cure me, for I know that Thou canst not love me and at the same time leave me in my misery." In another place she writes: "Treat with Our Lord with entire simplicity. Make Him the Depositary of all that you do or suffer. Offer Him all your actions, so that He may dispose of them according to His Will, uniting yourself to Him in all that you do, and in all that happens to you. Dwell in this adorable Heart; take all your small troubles, and all that is bitter, to Him: He will sweeten it all; there you will find the remedy for all your evils, strength in your weakness, and a refuge in every danger."

Jesus, True Friend of my heart! I thank Thee for the priceless gift of Friendship with Thyself that Thou hast deigned to offer me. I beg Thee to give me the grace of perfect fidelity to Thee, so that sacrificing myself generously in Thy service, I may be admitted to the intimacy of Thy love.

"Love Him, and keep Him for thy Friend, who when all go away, will not leave thee nor suffer thee to perish in the end."—(*Imit., Bk. II, chap. viii.*).

# XXXI

## HEART OF JESUS, OUR DIRECTOR AND OUR GUIDE

NO one can be a guide to himself: we need another to direct us in our journey through Life, and Our Lord knowing our need offers us Himself to conduct us safely home. The more completely I give myself up to His guidance, the more frequently and earnestly I call upon Him— "Show, O Lord, Thy ways to me, and teach me Thy paths. Direct me in Thy truth and teach me, for Thou art God my Saviour" (Ps. 24: 4-5)—the more swiftly will He lead me to my desired end.

Our Lord one day showed Himself to Saint Margaret Mary, and said to her: "I am thy Master Who will teach thee all that thou must do for My love." Whereupon the Saint was moved to write: "Let us look on the Heart of Jesus, as the Heart of our good Master, Who will teach us to know and love Him with all our strength and power, for in this love consists all our happiness."

To one of her friends who wrote and begged for advice, the Saint replied: "I confide you to the direction of the Sacred Heart of Jesus, so that He

Himself may be your Director and your Guide. He is all wise, and when we abandon ourselves wholly to His guidance and allow Him to act, He lets us make great progress in a short time without our being conscious of it, unless, indeed, we perceive it by the continual warfare which His grace makes upon our unmodified nature. He is such a good Director that in teaching us He gives us the means of accomplishing all He teaches—or else He does the work Himself."

"The Divine Heart of our Master will make known to you all the graces He reserves for you according to the measure of your fidelity to Him—fidelity especially among contradictions and humiliations which you ought to receive as pledges of His love. This is the way to please Him."

"My God, teach me Thou, and Thou alone! Direct me in Thy truth! Let not Thy voice be the passing word of a call or a command, but do Thou direct me! When I begin to take my feeble steps, direct me! When I hesitate, let me hear Thy comfortable word of exhortation! When I stumble and fall, speak to me that I may rise and take courage once more. In all my depression, my doubts, my cowardice, my ignorance, do thou, O my God, direct me! Guide me in every step through Life's hazards, till Thy Voice ceases and Thy Face appears." (*Bishop Hedley.*)

# XXXII

## HEART OF JESUS, OUR MEDIATOR

Ever pleading day and night,
Thou dost not from us part
O veiled and wondrous Sun,
O love of the Sacred Heart!

FROM the rising of the sun even to its setting, Our loving Lord offers Himself continually on our altars in the Holy Sacrifice of the Mass: unceasingly His Heart pleads with His Heavenly Father. "If any man sin," writes the Beloved Disciple, "we have an advocate with the Father, Jesus Christ the Just, and He is the propitiation for our sins; and not for ours only, but also for those of the whole world" (1 John 2); and St. Paul also, speaking of Our Lord as Mediator, says: "He is able also to save for ever them that come to God by Him, always living to make intercession for us." (Heb. 8:25)

When Jesus ascended into Heaven, He became our Advocate with the Eternal Father. There He continually holds out His wounded Hands in supplication for a sinful world. There He pours forth all the loving eloquence of His Heart in intercession for us. There

He prays unceasingly as of old on Calvary: "Father, forgive them for they know not what they do." There He pleads for us with the mighty love of His Heart. And not there only, for in the Tabernacle we have the same Most Sacred Heart, and from our altars and from the countless tabernacles of the world the same pleading ascends to the Throne of the Father. Nor is this all, for from the millions of human hearts into which Our Lord descends each day in Holy Communion, the same strong cry and supplication goes up.

From the midst of my heart, then, Jesus continues His pleading, each time I am united to Him in the Sacrament of His love. I have only to unite my prayers to His, to let my whispered supplication be caught up in the mighty music of His prayer, and through Him, and with Him, and in Him, I can obtain all I ask or need. "Make known to men," He said to Saint Margaret Mary, "that I ever stand in the presence of God the Father pleading on their behalf and if through human frailty, they are guilty of fault, I offer in their stead My own unblemished Heart."

Do I ever think of Our Lord thus pleading with me during the moments of Communion? If I did, should I not make better use of that priceless time? Should I not plead with Him more earnestly for sinners; for the multitudes that neither know nor love Him; for the sad and sorrow-stricken all over the world; for those in any danger of body or soul?  Should I not plead with Him more trustfully for my own needs, knowing that though I am sinful and unworthy to be heard, yet He, the All-Holy, is pleading for me?

O Christ, my Advocate, I join my prayer to Thine; I unite myself to all the pleadings of Thy Sacred Heart; I confide entirely in Thy goodness and in Thy love. Do Thou plead with the Father for me, a sinner, and for all sinners, that we may all praise and glorify Thee for ever in Heaven.

*Heart of Jesus, in Thee I trust!*

# XXXIII

## HEART OF JESUS,
## OUR JUDGE

SAINT Margaret Mary seems to have thought very specially of the Sacred Heart of Him Who was to be her Judge. It was this that sweetened the thought of Death for her. "O how sweet to die," she exclaimed, "after having had a constant devotion to Him Who is to be *our Judge!*" Remembrance of this sustained her when preparing for death, for we read in the notes of her last Retreat, July, 1690 : "O Heart of my Judge, do not deprive me for ever of Thy Love. As for the rest, do with me as Thou wilt; all I have, all I am, is Thine; all that I can do cannot repair the least of my faults; but for Thee, I am insolvent. Thou knowest it well, O my Divine Master. Put me in prison: I am willing, provided the prison be Thy Sacred Heart; and when I am there, keep me a close captive, held by the chains of Thy love, until I have paid Thee all that I owe Thee—and as I can never do this, so do I wish never to leave that prison."

When in Holy Communion Our Lord is united to me, I can do nothing better by way of preparation for my judgment than cast my whole care into His Sacred Heart. I can draw from the priceless treasures of His Heart wherewith to pay my debts. I can enter into His Heart, and shut myself up there like a criminal, who, out of regret and sorrow for the sins whereby he has angered his Judge, now desires to appease Him, and so encloses himself in this prison of love, so as to be there bound and fettered so securely that he has no more liberty except to love, even as love keeps our Judge captive in the Blessed Sacrament.

If, then, the thought of Death terrifies me, and if I fear to meet my Judge, my one safe refuge is His Heart. As Saint Margaret Mary writes in another place: "If you find yourself in an abyss of fear, go plunge yourself into the abyss of His Sacred Heart—and your fear will give place to love."

Jesus, my Lord, I adore Thee as my Judge. I own that I am utterly unworthy to lift up my eyes to Thee; yet, Lord, I not only come to Thee, but by Thy grace I am determined to leave Thee no more. "O Heart of love, I place all my trust in Thee, for though I fear all things from my weakness, I hope for all things from Thy mercy." I trust to Thee especially my death, and I trust to Thy Heart to receive me after death. My cause is safe if only Thou wilt judge me, not according to my iniquities, but according to Thy own most tender mercy. If Thou, O Lord, wilt observe iniquities, Lord, who shall endure it? But Thou wilt not forsake me, for my trust is wholly placed in the love of Thy Heart!

> O Sacred Heart!
> When Shades of Death shall fall,
> Receive us 'neath Thy gentle care,
> And save us from the tempter's snare;
> O Sacred Heart!
> O Sacred Heart!
> Lead exiled children home,
> When we may ever rest near Thee
> In peace and joy eternally,
> O Sacred Heart!
>
> *(Father F. Stanfield.)*

# LITANY OF THE
# SACRED HEART OF JESUS

*By a Decree (issued April, 1899) of the Sacred Congregation of Rites, the Litany of the Sacred Heart was approved for private and public use in the Universal Church.*

LORD, Have mercy on us. *Christ, have mercy on us.* Lord, have mercy on us.
Christ, hear us. *Christ, graciously hear us.*

God the Father of Heaven,

God the Son, Reedemer of the world,

God the Holy Ghost,

Holy Trinity, One God,

Heart of Jesus, Son of the Eternal Father,

Heart of Jesus, formed by the Holy Ghost in the womb of the Virgin Mary,

Heart of Jesus, hypostatically united to the Word of God,

Heart of Jesus, infinite in majesty,

Heart of Jesus, Holy Temple of God,

Heart of Jesus, Tabernacle of the most High,

Heart of Jesus, House of God, and Gate of Heaven,

Heart of Jesus, glowing furnace of charity,

Heart of Jesus, abode of justice and love,

*Have mercy on us.*

Heart of Jesus, full of kindness and love,

Heart of Jesus, abyss of all virtues,

Heart of Jesus, most worthy of all praise,

Heart of Jesus, King and centre of all hearts,

Heart of Jesus, wherein are all the treasures of wisdom and knowledge,

Heart of Jesus, wherein abides the fullness of the Godhead,

Heart of Jesus, in Which the Father was well pleased,

Heart of Jesus, of Whose fullness we have all received,

Heart of Jesus, desire of the eternal hills,

Heart of Jesus, patient and abounding in mercy,

Heart of Jesus, rich unto all that call upon Thee,

Heart of Jesus, Source of life and holiness,

Heart of Jesus, Atonement for our iniquities,

Heart of Jesus, glutted with reproaches,

Heart of Jesus, bruised for our sins,

Heart of Jesus, made obedient unto death,

Heart of Jesus, pierced by the lance,

Heart of Jesus, Source of all consolation,

Heart of Jesus, our life and resurrection,

Heart of Jesus, our peace and reconciliation,

Heart of Jesus, Victim of sin,

Heart of Jesus, Salvation of all who trust in Thee,

Heart of Jesus, Hope of all who die in Thee,

Heart of Jesus, delight of all the Saints,

*Have mercy on us.*

Lamb of God, Who takest away the sins of the world,
*Spare us, O Lord.*

Lamb of God, Who takest away the sins of the world,
*Graciously hear us, O Lord.*

Lamb of God, Who takest away the sins of the world,
*Have mercy on us.*

Jesus, meek and humble of Heart,
*Make our hearts like unto Thy Heart.*

## PRAYER

ALMIGHTY and Everlasting God, look upon the Heart of Thy well-beloved Son, and upon the praise and satisfaction which He rendered to Thee on behalf of sinners; and, being thus appeased, grant them the pardon which they seek from Thy mercy, in the name of the self-same Jesus Christ, Thy Son, Who liveth and reigneth with Thee, in the unity of the Holy Ghost, God for ever and ever.

*Amen.*

# FORM OF CONSECRATION TO THE MOST SACRED HEART OF JESUS

*Approved by Pope Leo XIII for public recital on the Feast of the Sacred Heart, June 11, 1899, on the Consecration of Mankind to the Most Sacred Heart of Jesus.*

O MOST sweet Jesus, Redeemer of mankind, behold us prostrate most humbly before Thy altar. To Thee we belong; Thine we wish to be; and that we may be united to Thee more closely, we dedicate ourselves each one of us to-day to Thy Most Sacred Heart.

Many have never known Thee; many, despising Thy commands, have rejected Thee. Have pity on them, most merciful Jesus, and draw all men to Thy Sacred Heart. Rule, O Lord, not only over the faithful who never have gone away from Thee, but also over the prodigal sons who have forsaken Thee; and make them return quickly to their Father's house, lest they perish of misery and hunger. Rule over those who have been misled by error, or separated by schism; and call them back to the haven of truth and the unity of faith, so that there may soon be one fold and one Shepherd. Lastly, rule over all who are sunk in the old superstition of the Gentiles, and vouchsafe to bring them out of darkness into the light and kingdom of God.

Give to Thy Church, O Lord, safety and sure liberty; give to all nations peace and order; and grant that, over the whole earth, from pole to pole, may resound the words: Praise be to the Divine Heart, through which was brought to us salvation; glory and honour be to It for ever. *Amen.*

# Consecration to the Sacred Heart

## Composed by Saint Margaret Mary

*(A rescript issued by Leo XIII, and dated January 13, 1898, attaches to the recitation of this Act 300 days' indulgence, once a day, applicable to the Souls in Purgatory.)*

I, N——, give and consecrate myself to the Sacred Heart of Our Lord Jesus Christ. I offer my person and my life, my actions, works, and sufferings, and it is my desire henceforth to use no part of my being save in honouring, loving, and glorifying Him. It is my steadfast purpose to belong only to Him, to do everything for love of Him, and to renounce absolutely all that could displease Him.

Therefore, I take Thee, O Sacred Heart, as the sole object of my love, as the protector of my life, as the safeguard of my salvation, and the remedy of my frailty and fickleness, for Thou canst make good all that I have done amiss, and Thou wilt be my sure refuge at the hour of my death. Be Thou, O loving Heart, my justification before God the Father, and turn aside from me His wrath, which I have so justly deserved. I put all my confidence in Thee, for I fear my own wickedness and weakness, and hope all from

Thy Goodness. Destroy in me all that may displease or oppose Thee. Let Thy pure love be so firmly impressed upon my heart that I may never forget Thee, and never be separated from Thee. I implore Thee of Thy mercy, suffer my name to be inscribed on Thy Heart, for I wish all my happiness and all my glory to consist in living and dying as Thy slave. *Amen.*

# Consecration to the Sacred Heart

## Composed by the Venerable Père de la Colombière

MY adorable Redeemer, I give and consecrate myself to Thy Sacred Heart in the fullest and most complete way of which I am capable. I have, as it were, nailed myself to Thy Cross by the vows of my profession. I renew them before Heaven and earth in this Divine Heart, and thank Thee for having inspired me to take these vows. I acknowledge that the yoke of Thy holy service is neither heavy nor burdensome, and that I am not weighed down by my bonds. So far am I from wishing to be released from them that I would fain multiply them and fasten the knots more closely.

Therefore I embrace the beloved cross of my vocation and will bear it until death; it shall be all my joy, my glory, and my delight. *"Absit mihi gloriari, nisi in Cruce Domini nostri Jesu Christi, per quem mihi mundus crucifixus est et ego mundo."* (God forbid that I should glory, save in the Cross of Our Lord Jesus Christ, by whom the world is crucified to me, and I to the world.—1 Gal. 6:14.)

God forbid that I should ever have any other treasure than His poverty, any other joys than His sufferings, any other love than Himself. My dearest Saviour, I will never abandon Thee; I will cling to none save to Thee; the narrowest paths of the perfect life to which I am called have no terrors for me, since Thou art my light and my strength.

I hope, therefore, O my Lord, that Thou wilt make me firm to resist all temptations, and victorious over the attacks of my enemies, and that Thou wilt stretch out over me Thy Hand which has already bestowed so many favours upon me, so that I may be yet further enriched.

By Thy Blood, by Thy Wounds, and by Thy Sacred Heart I implore Thee, O adorable Jesus, grant that by consecrating to Thee all that I am, I may this day become a new product of Thy love. *Amen.*

## Act of Consecration to the Most Sacred Heart of Jesus

*Composed and recited by the Servant of God, Mother Mary, of the Divine Heart Droste Zu Vischering, Religious of the Order of the Good Shepherd.*

MY most loving Jesus, I consecrate myself to-day anew and without reserve to Thy Divine Heart. To Thee I consecrate my body with all its senses, my soul with all its faculties, and my whole being. To Thee I consecrate all my thoughts, words, and works; all my sufferings and labours; all my hopes, consolations and joys; and, chiefly, I consecrate to Thee my poor heart that I may love but Thee, and be consumed as a victim in the flames of Thy love.

Accept, O Jesus, my most loving Spouse, the desire that I have to console Thy Divine Heart and to belong to Thee for ever. Take possession of me in such a manner that henceforward I may have no other liberty than that of loving Thee.

In Thee I place unbounded confidence, and I hope for the pardon of my sins from Thine infinite mercy. In Thy hands I lay all my cares, and principally that of my eternal salvation. I promise to love Thee and to honour Thee, until the last moment of my life, and as far as I am able to propagate devotion to Thy Most Sacred Heart.

Dispose of me, O Divine Heart of Jesus, according to Thy good pleasure. I desire no other recompense than Thy greater glory and Thy holy love.

Grant me the grace to find in Thy Most Sacred Heart my dwelling-place; there I desire to pass each day of my life; there I wish to breathe forth my last sigh. Do Thou also make my heart Thy abode and the place of Thy repose, that so we may remain intimately united, until one day I may praise, love, and possess Thee for all eternity, and sing for ever the infinite mercies of Thy Most Sacred Heart. *Amen.*

*(Pope Leo XIII, by a Decree of the Sacred Congregation of Indulgences, dated January 7, 1903, deigned to grant an Indulgence of 300 days—applicable also to the dead—to be gained once a day by all the faithful, who, with contrite heart, shall devoutly recite the above Act of Consecration to the Most Sacred Heart of Jesus.*

## Prayer of Saint Margaret Mary

ETERNAL Father, suffer me to offer Thee the Heart of Jesus Christ, Thy Beloved Son, as He Himself offered It in sacrifice to Thee. Receive this offering for me, as well as all the desires, sentiments, affections, movements, and acts of this Sacred Heart. They are all mine since He offered Himself for me, and henceforth I wish to have no other desires than His. Receive them in satisfaction for my sins, and in thanksgiving for all Thy benefits. Grant me through His merits all the graces necessary for my salvation, especially that of final perseverance. Receive them as so many acts of love, adoration and praise, which I offer to Thy Divine Majesty, since it is through the Heart of Jesus that Thou art worthily honoured and glorified. *Amen.*

## Invocations of the Most Sacred Heart

### Composed by Saint Margaret Mary

HEART of my Jesus, save me.
Heart of my Creator, perfect me.
Heart of my Saviour, deliver me.
Heart of my Judge, pardon me.
Heart of my Father, govern me.
Heart of my Spouse, love me.
Heart of my Master, teach me.
Heart of my King, rule me.
Heart of my Benefactor, enrich me.
Heart of my Shepherd, guard me.
Heart of my Friend, caress me.
Heart of the Infant Jesus, attract me.
Heart of Jesus dying on the Cross, pay my debts.
Heart of Jesus, give Thyself to me.
Heart of my Brother, stay with me.
Heart of unspeakable goodness, pardon me.
Most loving Heart, unite Thyself with me.
Most kind Heart, live in me.
Most merciful Heart, answer for me.

Most humble Heart, repose in me.
Most patient Heart, endure me.
Most faithful Heart, abide with me.
Most noble Heart, bless me.
Most peaceful Heart, calm me.
Most perfect Heart, ennoble me.
Most Sacred Heart, preserve me.
Most Holy Heart, make me holy.
Most blessed Heart, cure me.
Most tender Heart, be merciful to me.
Heart of Jesus Who understandest me, console me.
Divine Heart of Jesus, strengthen me.
Most dear Heart, call me to Thee, and never permit
me to be separated from Thee. *Amen.*

# Invocations to the Sacred Heart

P ROFOUND adoration of the Heart of Jesus,
Ardent love of the Heart of Jesus,
Fervent zeal of the Heart of Jesus,
Reparation of the Heart of Jesus,
Thanksgiving of the Heart of Jesus,
Assured confidence of the Heart of Jesus,
Fervent prayer of the Heart of Jesus,
Humility of the Heart of Jesus,
Eloquent silence of the Heart of Jesus,
Obedience of the Heart of Jesus,
Meekness and Peace of the Heart of Jesus,
Ineffable bounty of the Heart of Jesus,
Universal charity of the Heart of Jesus,
Profound recollection of the Heart of Jesus,
Suffering and sacrifice of the Heart of Jesus,
Infinite patience of the Heart of Jesus,
Interior of the Heart of Jesus,
Resignation of the Heart of Jesus,

*I unite myself to Thee.*

Desires, intentions and will of the Heart of Jesus,
    I unite myself to you.
Love of the Heart of Jesus, inflame my heart.

Charity of the Heart of Jesus, fill my heart.

Strength of the Heart of Jesus, sustain my heart.

Mercy of the Heart of Jesus, pardon my heart.

Patience of the Heart of Jesus, tire not of my heart.

Reign of the Heart of Jesus, establish Thyself in my heart.

Science of the Heart of Jesus, teach my heart.

Will of the Heart of Jesus, dispose of my heart.

Zeal of the Heart of Jesus, inflame my heart.

O Immaculate Virgin, pray to the Sacred Heart of Jesus for us.

# OFFERING OF THE HOUR OF GUARD

**D**IVINE Jesus, my most sweet Saviour! I offer Thee this Hour of Guard, during which in union with (*here name the patron of your hour*), I desire to love and to glorify Thee, and, above all, to console Thy adorable Heart for the forgetfulness and ingratitude of mankind. Accept, I beseech Thee, for this end, all my thoughts, words, actions, and sufferings; above all receive my heart, which I give Thee without reserve, entreating Thee to consume it in the fire of Thy pure love. *Amen.*

## ACT OF OBLATION

ECCE, *venio!* Behold I come! O sweetest Jesus, Divine Lamb, perpetually sacrificed upon our Altars for the salvation of the world, I desire to unite myself to Thee, to suffer with Thee, and to immolate myself like Thee. To this end I offer Thee the sufferings, trials, humiliations, and crosses which Thy Divine Providence has strewn on my path; I offer them to Thee for the intentions with which Thy Sacred Heart offers and immolates Itself.

May my feeble sacrifice be acceptable to Thee, and obtain blessings for the Church, the world, and all poor sinners. Deign to accept it through the hands of Mary, and in union with the immolation of her Immaculate Heart. *Amen.*

## ACT OF REPARATION

HEART of Jesus in the Eucharist, sweet
companion in our exile,
Heart solitary, Heart humiliated,
Heart abandoned, Heart forgotten,
Heart despised, Heart outraged,
Heart ignored by men.
Heart, lover of our hearts,
Heart desirous of being loved,
Heart patient in waiting for us,
Heart longing to be prayed to,
Heart source of new graces,
Heart wrapped in silence desiring to speak to souls,
Heart, the sweet refuge of the hidden life,
Heart, teacher of the secrets of union with God,
Heart of Him who sleeps, yet ever watches,
Eucharistic Heart of Jesus, have pity on us.
Jesus victim, I desire to console Thee;
I unite myself to Thee, and sacrifice myself with Thee;
I annihilate myself in Thy presence;
I would forget myself to be mindful of Thee;
I would be forgotten and despised for love of Thee;

*I adore Thee, Eucharistic Heart of Jesus.*

And be neither understood nor loved unless by Thee;
I will silence myself to listen to Thee;
I will abandon myself to lose myself in Thee.
Grant that I may thus appease Thy thirst,
The thirst for my sanctification and salvation,
And that being purified I may bestow on Thee a pure
and true love.
I would not longer weary Thy patience; take possession
of me.
I give myself to Thee.
I offer Thee all my actions, my intellect to be illumi-
nated by Thee, my heart to be guided by Thee,
my will to be made strong, my soul and body to be
nourished, my misery to be lightened.
Eucharistic Heart of my Jesus, whose blood is the life
of my soul, may it be no longer I that live, but do
Thou alone live in me. *Amen.*

*(Indulgence of 200 days every time this Act of Reparation
is made.)*

Additional titles available from

# St. Augustine Academy Press
Books for the Traditional Catholic

## Titles by Mother Mary Loyola:

Blessed are they that Mourn
Confession and Communion
Coram Sanctissimo (Before the Most Holy)
First Communion
First Confession
Forgive us our Trespasses
Hail! Full of Grace
Heavenwards
Sursum Corda! (An Anthology of Short Works)
Home for Good
Jesus of Nazareth: The Story of His Life Written for Children
The Child of God: What comes of our Baptism
The Children's Charter
The Little Children's Prayer Book
The Soldier of Christ: Talks before Confirmation
Trust
Welcome! Holy Communion Before and After
With the Church, Volumes I and II

## Titles by Father Lasance:

The Catholic Girl's Guide
The Young Man's Guide

## Tales of the Saints:

A Child's Book of Saints by William Canton
A Child's Book of Warriors by William Canton
Legends & Stories of Italy by Amy Steedman
Mary, Help of Christians by Rev. Bonaventure Hammer
The Book of Saints and Heroes by Leonora Lang
Saint Patrick: Apostle of Ireland
The Story of St. Elizabeth of Hungary by William Canton

Check our Website for more:
www.staugustineacademypress.com